AN EXPERIENCE ON THE TONGUE

Glen Wilson

Doire Press

First published in 2019

Doire Press
Aille, Inverin
Co. Galway
www.doirepress.com

Layout: Lisa Frank
Cover design: Tríona Walsh
Cover image: Ant_art / Shutterstock.com
Author photo: Joanne Symmington

Printed by Clódóirí CL
Casla, Co. na Gaillimhe

ISBN 978-1-907682-67-4

We gratefully acknowledge the assistance of The Arts Council of Northern Ireland.

LOTTERY FUNDED

CONTENTS

(II) The Lotus Gait

(IV) The Founds

For Rhonda, Sian and Cain,
I am truly blessed to have you all in my life.

(I) Wordless But All Verb

Once Upon a Time

Nestled in the backseat
of a Maroon Lada Estate,
wrapped in a kingsize quilt

my brother and I stared out
the windows and sketched our breaths
on the cold damp glass.

We drew dragons fighting knights
with out-of-proportion swords,
scenes that would never resolve.

Boys go to sleep, Mum said
as she tried to fight the weight
pushing down her own eyelids.

We waited parked up on the kerb
as Dad said goodnight to his friend
huddled in a squat concrete tower,

and as a family we set off,
stealing prohibited moments
along abandoned Armagh roads.

I tried to listen in as my parents
shared the contents of their day
in hushed conversation.

Bomb scare on Woodhouse street…
a break-in at Castle Hardware,
Fletcher rang in sick again…

Nothing out of the ordinary.

The town zips past in quickly turned pages,
as the moon and stars seem to remain
slow to change and motion.

Then the trees come reaching out in
truncated tragedy, held by their stoic
boughs and relentless roots.

I look at my brother who is already over,
mouth gaping open for dreams to take
full command with their gossamer grip.

I don't remember being carried
back into the house, only waking
amongst Paddington Bear wallpaper.

Orchard County

Death and life are in the power of the tongue:
and they that love it shall eat the fruit thereof.

                                        — *Proverbs 18:21*

The two of us shouldn't be here,
chasing each other through the perfect lines
of Bramley apple trees, where the fruit is ripe,
just needing a gentle twist to release.

We had jumped the hedge in the dusk,
having watched the summer workers leave,
something to do to score off a list:
a lust, a fantasy, a frisson of trust.

We tear the fruit down, eat and look long
at the bitten cores, naked they glow, before
becoming modest so very fast. As we gather up
our harvest of skinned ego a voice shouts:

Who is there?

We run, stain and scrape ourselves
as we go through the sheugh
to make our escape. An aftertaste
we don't recognise loiters on our tongues.

Gavage

Brains the size of a pea
my father told me the first time
he shoved a feeding tube down
a young gosling's throat. I feel
the machine whirring into life,
the clank and then the steady hum
of corn and boiled fat mush
racing down into the bird's belly.

We had an average clutch then,
the numbers have grown considerably,
less hands-on too, we've bred them
to be more amenable. One gander
after another strain towards me, opening beaks,
eager to expand oesophagi,
they keep swallowing,
they must enjoy it.

Through the skylight I watch
a skein of Branta geese,
honking as they switch positions
in their flying V just ahead
of a rising plane. I wish I could
escape to the winter sun.

Mouths to Feed

He smiled while he did it, laughing almost
as the burlap wriggled
and bunched beneath calloused hands,
red with the cold, clad with dark clay.

My brother and I watched from the bedroom
as our uncle made his way down towards
the brook, the collie padding along behind,
cowed by his master's stride.

I remember finding them the day before,
the soft mewls of discovery, the furred circles
of movement, the runs of ginger markings
on white, but with claws sharp enough to wound.

It would have been better to have left them,
he said, when we carried them back
in an old cardboard box, my aunt sneaking us
a saucer of milk and an old scarf.

She is down the hall in the kitchen now,
we hear her scrubbing the pots and pans,
she has been working on them for half an hour,
they will gleam later, her hands raw.

He came back ten minutes later,
the sack neat, folded. He hung it up on a hook
to be used again. The mother cat met him,
purred and stroked past his shins.

Angelshare

I love the sound of the column stills,
always have. I started in the distillery
on the first of July, everything outside
honey-soaked, the grass singed yellow.
An apprentice to dark rooms, my nerves
quietened by the comfort of low flames,
where fermented grain-mash burned in
charred white oak casks, a magic tamed.
The scent never changed though they measure
the spirit by decimal points instead of rule
of thumb. I see those first coopers like vapours
bending metal hoops to embrace the wood,
handling conflagrations into armistice
so it matures enough to be poured out gold.
Whiskey, the Gaelic word for water anglicised,
sits on the lips, roughs the throat smooth.
Against the grain of ancient casks hauled
from the mouths of Spanish shipwrecks,
this taut hand-to-slack-hand journey
mellows the fluid to a palatable proof, distils
it to a single sip, a sensation. That is what I am,
what we all are, an experience on the tongue,
casting off from the world, hoping the taste
gilt-edged, worth gifting on.

Blue Strings Easton

The bicycle wheels' click-clack progress
along Tirnascobe Road told us he was passing by,
tweed jacket, tweed flat cap, a biblical beard.

I don't recall who told me his name first,
as if it too appeared from nowhere, like the blue strings
that were tied to every thing he owned.

He didn't have much, off the electric grid,
his house had a simplicity to it. We reckoned
he would be away for at least an hour so sneaked inside.

Stood to attention along a solitary cupboard
were clear bottles with a strong smelling drink,
in the corner lay his homebrew stills.

In the other corner a dusty wooden crib, above it
a painting of a wren in flight, a forest in the distance,
wings never destined to reach a nest.

The windows had no glass just murky plastic sheets
to keep out the wind that billowed inward
and out like a scientific model of smoker's lungs.

A fire glowed low, calmed by the piled-up slack,
the only other furniture was a plain table and chair,
a still life disturbed by the oscillating light.

On the table sat a chunk of wood and a whittling knife,
sharp enough to birth some image solid. On its handle
yet another blue string, edges strained and frayed.

He's coming back!

I was the last out the door and there he was,
legs resting on the road as he sat on his bicycle,
watching us flee. I caught his gaze, eyes of blue weight,

circled with a deep-knowing red.
We kept turning round to see if he was following,
always expecting but never seeing him again.

A Line of Hawthorns

(i) Peter John, Autumn 1998, New Forge College

I break the spine and each page is a turning
over of soil, new descriptions and terms
for movements of a second nature, relearning
ridge and furrow in black and white.
I measure pH balances, soil composition,
then picture sods of grass that the tractor spins up
from my father's lower fallow field. I know
which earth crumbles, which holds its shape.

I see my father getting down from the tractor cab,
his eye his plumb line as he charts the angle,
adjusts the tread as if to say, *We'll start here.*
Years have refined and exaggerated the process.
But the action is still the ploughshare following
the coulter.

(ii) John Isaac, Spring 1980, Gortin

Listen to the Ewes singing February songs, Son!
I hear him saying still as I insulate the barn
with tightly packed bales and twine.

They huddle together, their coats grown
back from being sheared six months ago.
I check for udder growth, a mother's swelling.

I see the first ewe ready to go, search for
the beginning of legs. I tie small cotton cords
to his feet to help pull the lamb out.

He must play his part and shake his head
to rupture the membrane. And he does,
pushing through virgin limbs slick and wet.

I wipe the mucus from his nose, slap the ribs
to start the lungs, glad when he breathes in
the slurry-tinged air, wanting more.

I help him suckle with syringe, a twelve-inch
rubber tube delivering colostrum milk directly
into his never-to-be-empty-again stomach.

The ewe starts to nurse in the lambing jug,
I take painting irons, brand them with the family
colour, I hear the rising bleating of the next.

She watches me from the kitchen door
hand on the small of her back to ease
the pressure, spine arched with hope

after last year's loss.

(iii) Jacob, Winter 1951, McVeigh's Bar

He liked his drink, pressed glass to pursed lips
was his natural state, and tonight I was going
to keep him there, never letting the whiskey
grains settle long enough to burn. I owned
only an acre of land but made much of it, cadging
the best seeds, borrowing materials from the corners
of other fields, especially his. I have a few ewes
but he has plenty, Father made sure of that.

Blessed by what a piece of paper gave him
he *really* should pay attention to the sheughs
and ditches of fine print. He signs his name,
I take it, slip it inside my windcheater and leave,
hear him order a hotpot from the girl who
would've been his wife but ended up being mine.

Taking Soup

We have been standing here long enough to see
that the ladle was engraved *Sheffield Steel.*

The missionaries had come to the town, handing out
a few loaves with promises of more if we would follow.

We had left while it was still dark and were on the road
before our neighbours would be up for morning mass.

Sean O'Kelly had already told me what he thought.
'I won't have anything to do with *them,* John!'

I had helped him bury his youngest just five days ago
among many fresh mounds of earth at the graveyard.

The queue moves slowly even with seven servers
filling up the misshapen bowls with a slivery broth.

The man from the mission gives us some tracts, words
we can't read and looks solemnly at Briege's rosary beads.

She lays them down in a bucket near the hall door,
says goodbye to these pearls of a *Babylonian Whore.*

Mary McElmurray helps her husband towards a table,
dragging his gammy leg, she turns to me and nods

before quickly looking away. We had been something once.
But they were other people, children from another parish.

It comes to my turn and I let the steam rise into my nostrils,
feel the warmth trickle down my parched throat.

A young girl hands me a hunk of bread, *Bless you*, she says,
I chew wildly until my jaw aches and watch my children eat.

Soup dribbles through the bristles on my chin; I slurp sacrilege
and new sacraments with the same grateful tongue.

The Stable

The thin rod of metal twisted into a handle
swings loosely in my grip as the lamp's yellow
makes reachable lines in the dark yard.

The stable door is ajar; her own light like a firefly
gives away her movement; I'm glad to find her.
I lift the latch and secure the door behind me.

Having heard me she has gone and hid, her lamp
extinguished, hung on a nail above two tin buckets,
Carol, Carol, I call, laughing as my voice echoes.

Only one horse is in here now, an obedient mare
that only stirs as I step past her stall. I scratch behind
her ear, her hair needs brushed — Carol usually does this.

I often watch her without her knowing, she smiles
and talks to the horses as she pulls the brush through
tangles, making them one flowing mane of hair.

I search the other stalls, knock horseshoes off hooks,
they clatter loudly in my good ear. She isn't here
perhaps slipping out when I was distracted.

I pass the light over my wrist to check my watch,
see now the wrinkled forearm, liver-spotted
with a sparse grey down and look back at the house.

The kitchen lights are off, I remember now
where she has gone.

The Gamekeeper

Bowed with his red cowlick quiff, snagged with spores,
so thin his coat bends in on him, cheekbones sucked tight.

I tackled him hard, his breeches are torn by brambles,
dark bloodied knees glisten in the moonlight.

I swing my torch and notice his boots: one black, one brown,
the tongues of both opening up as if to complain.

I see the two pheasants at his feet, strangled
with cord, necks twisted round each other,

lovers perhaps in life or victims of circumstance,
possibly both. A decent haul for a night's poaching.

I pick them up, separate the limp bodies, throw one back.
I lower the shotgun and motion back towards the village.

He looks at me then gathers the bird, crossing himself
he limps off, fallen branches cracking as he goes.

The maid answers the kitchen door at the big house,
she nods as I hand her the recovered game and leave.

I skin a coney I caught earlier, the pot boils with
freshly drawn water, dawn touches all the windows.

The Seed Fiddler's Broadcast

I calibrate the lever to tune it up,
setting number two sows six pints
of Clover Seed per statute acre.

These rills of Tyrone's heaped earth,
these depressions to be filled,
loosen in anticipation of seed-song.

Oil the journals and grease the stick well.
There is much to put in before life yields,
the rendition of many seasons.

Set the machine to your walk.
These fields are the audience,
every inch waits to hear me play.

My steps disturb the surface,
just enough for the future to reverberate
in the clearance of the past.

I scatter the seed like notes of a scale
until all the soil sings with this music,
the harvest will be all beautiful refrain —

Keep your seed clean, keep the belt tight.

* Lines in italics taken from the instructions for 'The Aero Broadcaster and Seed Sower'.

Pipping

Too big now to be content
to breathe through the pores of the shell,
the cry comes
from a muscle on the back of its neck,
swinging the egg tooth forward;
wordless but all verb,
the shell gives way.
Calcium carbonate fragments
fall out into mosaic;
how quickly these walls
of protection, then prison, fall,
see how thin
and easily breakable they are.
The egg tooth
is lost soon after hatching,
look closely and you can see
where it once was,
and remember
its latent strength.

Opening the Gates

A rag of white hung on the rails,
a small fleck of blood at the corner
where the t-shirt had ripped.

What drew them to the park at night?
I drag my litter picker
and bag of refuse sacks inside.

They have set one of the bins
on fire, another is sprayed
Freedom in dark green.

One of the tundra swans calls,
whoo-whoo, three dappled chicks
waddle under her wings.

I almost don't see him, the cob,
as the tall reeds sway, as if
they could claim him.

His neck lies a half-heart
in brown leaves, crisp packets
and a crushed Harp can.

Canis Lupus

For her to urinate for the first time
I must massage her tummy, my pink heat words
summoning her insides to flow. She whines
but eventually wets the dirt. I don't know
why I know this, perhaps a flinch of memory
made me lick the soft down.

We are all rooted in touch,
the passing-on of thoughts
by staggering steps. I cannot
tell her how to hunt, she must see
the hare upright, nose twitching,
gambling on scent.

She must track the lines I take,
notice how I stay upwind of my prey until
I can court closer than a lover. She must see
how deep to bite for life, how far up
the teeth the blood paints, how two rhythms
must become one.

I help her learn how the throat forms
the words and the breath pushes up
the volume. We howl and that
is our culmination, announcing
we are here, surviving, overcoming
the hurt and the fight.

I lie down and watch her chew and play
with the last of our dinner, an only child,
the runt that endured the rest of the litter.
I notice the creases in my own fur
tongue-shaped, tufted up almost sharp,
a killer's pattern, a mother's stroke.

Proof of Life

Cowpat-crusted boots nudge the door open,
in come the brothers, John and James Magee.
James is taller but John does all the talking.

Here to collect the bounty reward, Constable.

James holds up the tangle of matted orange fur,
an April draft wags them as if they were still
hunting, running out there in the woods.

From behind the mesh I point towards the hatch,
I think we must have caught a litter, John laughs
as he wretches the mother fox's jaws open.

James pulls the spine-covered tongue down,
slices it off, exsanguinated, only a little tear
of blood, all she has to say, spots the linoleum.

I tally them as he slaps the tongues on the counter,
thin rashers of bacon on the turn, fifty-pence a tongue,
evidence of the cull, logged in a black and red ledger.

Zion

Every time we heard distant footfall
we thought we were found,
only to have our number swell.
We rolled over, offered sanctuary
to half-brothers and step-sisters
in this game of hide-and-seek.

To pass the time we pieced together
the discarded refrains of nursery rhymes,
Jack and Jill went up the Hill...
when the wind blows the cradle will rock...
A-tishoo! A-tishoo! We all fall down.
Did no one hear our choir sing?

One time curious boys peered down
into our den only to be spooked
by our open arms, our fetid familiarity.
Later a dark figure loomed over us,
reciting rites in the habitual Latin,
as if to seal the place in time.

Now we watch the blue marquee sky
rise up, rippling until it is taut,
this is our homecoming.
Unaccustomed to such rapt attention
we are blinded by the heavenly lights
as faceless angels in white retrieve us.

They match up our bones,
jigsaw puzzles on tarpaulin,
finally fleshed out
in the promise of new bodies,
tender names in white,
the truth of us delivered.

(II) The Lotus Gait

The Lotus Gait

Mother is in the kitchen pretending to cook dinner,
I can hear her flat feet shuffling on the cold earth,
see her shadow flit at the bottom of the door. I bite my lip.

Grandmother sits outside rocking my brother
to sleep, he hasn't slept a night fully through yet,
sometimes to calm him I let him suck my finger.

My aunt holds up a pair of Lotus shoes, embroidered
with peacock feathers, a gift from my betrothed,
the youngest son of a great Han family from the city.

She does an elegant turn, shows me how one day
I too can walk like her, swaying towards balance,
bending the knee to make such small steps.

She hands me a rolled cloth to bite down on,
steadies herself as each bone snaps — the last thing
I see before I pass out is my toes curling into my sole.

I wake and she is there, tightening a bandage
soaked in goat blood and herbs over my feet,
covering all the purpling skin in deft figure eights.

I'm told Emperor Li Yu was so entranced
by his beloved's elegant dance in white silken feet
all the other courtesans ran to copy her,

seeking advancement, slowing their stride.

Vashti

He has asked me to dance,
a peer-shamed suggestion,
a wine-slurred wager on beauty,
a peacock's swagger.
The concubines all look to me,
the thin veils we wear
make all our eyes diamonds
searching for reflection.
I tell the servant *No*.
He is disappointed but understands
and scuttles off to relay the news,
knowing he will sup of the King's wrath first.
I can imagine my husband
because I have felt his kingdom-crushing hand
and though perfumed by his violence,
I know where the line is and who draws it.

Finding the Water Cold

Neats tongues about her necke
Were hung in open show;
And thus unto the cucking stoole
This famous Scould did goe.

         — "The Cucking of a Scould"*

It took five strong men to raise her up
then lower her down into the frigid river,

even the slightest of waifs was heavier
coming out of the fast-flowing Erne.

The second time she rose back up her garments
were skin tight, provocative in her very shaming.

The oak creaked as the men's hands chafed
on the rope, all of Belturbet cheered

as the young woman's underwear was torn away
by the relentless current.

The whole town watched it sail downstream,
an undulating map of pure white.

*The cucking stool was used as a punishment for women for offences such as talking back or scolding and in some cases sexual offences, such as prostitution or bearing a child out of wedlock.

A Young Boy Gathers Sugar, Lancashire 1770

The act flecks shards, candies my eyes,
dusts my labour, they are having guests
at the big house tonight and want to impress.

My sister says they make apples, carrots,
pies from sugar, dyed to look like the real thing
until they are bitten into and the sugar hits.

The cook raps my knuckles when she finds me
taking the odd crumb from the floor.
But she does not rap them too hard.

I saw a slave once through the window;
hems overlong, sleeves not covering his forearms,
he held his master's accounts in a leather folio.

There to see the mill owner, they discuss
business above all our heads as the day
progresses around us in busy toil.

I set down the sugar nips, lick my fingers
sweetened raw with effort, covered
in what I could not afford, a taste,

a sliver of a distant world.

Marie Tussaud Preserves the Line of Succession

The Incorruptible he was called,
his head nodding to decay on my table,
beside paintpots, brushes, a crust of bread.
It started when the King's pate was whisked
from his place of prominence in our window
by a draft blowing from the guillotine.
Pikes paraded past, jaunting up and down,
topped with slack faces, expressions undecided
between comedy and tragedy. Until they turned
they were competition for business,
mouths speaking cadaverine words
that filled up every chamber with their rhetoric.
Suitors would come in every few months
and present the faces of the beaten rivals,
asking me to preserve their victory
in wax and dyes and wigs. I simply had to wait
for those conquerors to follow next,
fresh blood adds to the coats of red staining the floor.
It was hard to replicate the strands of hair,
they yellow easily. I smooth them over
so the scalp is covered, it is close enough.
I flesh my next design and add it to the frame,
taking and removing as it starts to take shape,
holding the unblinking gaze as long as I can.

Mary Richardson Sees Herself in the Mirror of Venus

Velázquez's 'Rokeby Venus' hangs in full view,
passed as a wedding gift from Dukes to Lords,
kept in private collections in private rooms
until it was given its brazen space here,
a national treasure, blessed among all women.

A cherub holds the frame she, and also us
are meant to see ourselves in; naked but chaste,
wings too small to cover great distance.
Her back is to us, facing glass
and the half-draped red velvet sheet.

Beauty must self-flagellate; the inch-thick glass
cracks in all directions, I cut lines into her back,
the top of her thigh, a cruel wound in the neck.
I use a weapon with a keen edge, a meat cleaver
to hack an emancipated pound of flesh.

I watch a constable slip as he runs towards me
on the freshly polished floor. Six, seven slashes
of protest before she could be dressed with a silk robe.
Did I strike deep enough? Too much?
Passion is the worst seamstress but it is all the talent I have.

Their answer is to keep parcels, muffs and satchels
stowed with the umbrellas and canes. They fear
someone breaking the difference between art
and audience. My hands are cuffed behind me,
but I can still feel the thrum of the giddy cleaver.

The Bridesmaids of Passchendaele

When Helen is leading the shift, the conversation
is reserved but Kate encourages the bawdy song,
so we canaries sing as the steel pineapples move.

We share a lot of *Did-you-hear-about-so-and-so*,
laughter and silences. Mock admonishments
percolate the relentless, roiling clatter.

Amy, Sarah and I were in the same class at school
just last year, all but two of the boys in that room
went to the front, seven have already returned.

Last month Cybil was blinded by a Mills bomb
wired wrong. I watched her sight bleed into her palm.
She came back two months later, unlike Agnes.

I can still see her shoes poking out from under
that blanket. A thick khaki blanket veiled her body
as crimson wept from where her head used to be.

Judy Smith works steadily at the end of the line,
quiet with thoughts of the battles to win,
when her war has already been lost.

Amy talks endlessly about her Jim heading off,
catches herself off the edge of the workbench,
she rubs her rib-pronounced belly.

Jaundiced eyes stream out at closing time,
hurrying back past the street lights —
signal fires sporadic in their return each day.

Amy picks a rose as we walk to the bus stop, slips
it into my yellowed blouse to cover up the acrid
scent of copper and add a splash of welcome red.

Sarah's boots catch in the mud of the ditch,
it takes all of us to hoist her out, laughing we link arms,
march towards the approaching omnibus.

Mutabilis

They grow us in large numbers,
pruned to the preferred shape,
they have keen eyes and secateurs
that judge quick,
there is profit in a cloned beauty,
bowed to their sharp templates of worship.

They have many names for us:
Unique Blanche,
White Provence,
Rosa Unica,
Lactea
and others depending on the tongue.

They wear the same gloves as their fathers,
numbing the points,
the vivacious power of our thorns,
whispering practised lines to tell us how much
we mean to them,
to swell our bloom.

The cards given to us say:
clear and sweet
with light notes of honey,

a singular fragrance.

The Saffron Gatherers of Santorini

They pick with a balance
of strength and lightness of touch,
the crocus copper
colouring fingertips
as they pinch the stamens
with both hands.
This is a harvest for the rich
so they dress accordingly,
jewelled and cut to status
but perfumed with a willing sweat.
Why this scene
committed to fresco
and not any other?
Perhaps this was one pure moment
that the artist found,
no wars, no salting the earth,
no debt-ridden
words of dead men
dictating the future.
Instead it is two women
gathering in saffron,
extending themselves
and in that labour,
its own pleasure.

Vesuvius Speaks

The horses felt it first,
a once-placid mare
kicked the doors clean off her stall,
one of the slaves grabbed the leather reins
and was dragged for a half mile
before, scuffed and torn,
he gave up on her
and hobbled back towards the stables.

When the tower of smoke cut itself into the sky,
it spewed copious dark words over the city,
coating everyone with the spit
that forced itself upon us,
well past the point of forbearance.

Ash fell on the forum,
the baths,
the brothels,
every eloquent word
and guttural moan silenced.

We watched from across the bay.
Some struggled even at this distance to admit
it was clinging to their cloaks,
nestling between pumiced toes,
making all complicit.

An Eurasian Magpie Sees the Coast of Lesbos

Amongst the others it is all noisy chattering,
black and white plumage for the show,
every one bringing back a steady silver flow
of coin, crumpled foil and tarnished ring.
All that we have is stolen from those before:
we built roof nests like our mothers, prey
like our fathers, beaks twisting the day
into having a little something more.

Hello Mr Magpie, how's your wife and kids?
a stranger says to me as we are brought ashore
clutching the cross and chain you once wore.
I could curse him but instead close my eyelids
to see the settling of your iridescent skin,
long green-gloss tails, parallel to the wind.

Under Olive Nets, Greek Border, August 2015

Arman has climbed a tree to keep watch.
Two days ago the border guards came close,
near enough that we could see their faces
but they could not yet see ours.
      Barakat sleeps on a pillow of smooth rock,
the hardest thing is comfortable if you adapt yourself to it.
Where light stumbles in the grove
I see ants march in line to the fallen crumbs
of the biscuits we had for dinner last night,
happy in their industry, they are oblivious
to how anyone could wipe them out with one kick.
      I reach up and pick a ripe olive and squeeze
until the oil trickles down and pools in my palm.
      I wish I could swim in its golden span
but it dries quickly into the skin.
I run my fingers through sea-salted
and sun-bleached hair,   there are no mirrors
only the shimmers of shallow rivers
to tell us what we look like;
      we are defined by ripples,
decisions made by others far away
swelled to unforeseen waves
      by the time they broke against us.

Grief is waking from a nightmare to find out it is all true
and you cannot let the memory dissipate like gas,
      and night is a taut bedsheet pressing down, suffocating
      and, when I wriggle out I find there is no one there.
      It is finding the person you thought you were
halved but kept together by a dull necessity
of flesh and blood and bones and duty.
      It is time to go Arman shouts,
I stir Barakat and we run again.
Behind us the net billows up like a figure,

struggling to surface
       and follow us through the gaps.
There are ghosts of us
       left at each place we've rested,
charred voids of families reaching out,
       unable to stretch further
       than the last person they touched.

Show and Tell

It's been forty-one nights since
I was in my own bed and Aleppo
feels like another person's film.

We were two doors away
from where the first bombs exploded,
one demon summons others,
saints are chased from holy places,
forgotten altars are blooded again.

When I was a child I needed stitches
from banging my head against a wall,
now, the wall is no longer there.

We drove to the next town
then the next town,
as they fell like dominoes
our numbers growing, but thinning as well.

I got separated from my father,
a rebel soldier told me to run
for *they* would be here soon.

I left a message for father
Head towards Germany.

My hand shook as I chalked my name.
I had been training to be a teacher.

Spoon Feeding

Here now, this is what
I want to tell you,
see this sentence
it's sup —
posed to jar
like thick strawberry jam
spilling down your front.
There now, I'll wipe that up
don't want you to miss
a single bit.
Do you like it?
What do you mean you don't know what it's about?
It's about the Iraq War, silly!

The Spectacles

They are piled up, differing dioptres, myopic
and farsighted alike, the accumulation
of corrective lenses. They once saw things,
saw them in detail, in measurable horror.

They focussed through jagged glass,
crystals of their world scattered, nothing
left to stop a murkier world marching in,
bridges were warped by the acrid smell.

Bent thin legs that held vision in place
twist and wrap around each other.
The temple pieces are broken with no ear
to listen to the scripture they once carried.

Tortoise shell, horn-rimmed, gold, silver,
plastic, each one bends the light now.
Generations pass by the mount of spectacles,
add their curious breath, mist up the lens.

I take a cloth, wipe, make the glass clear,
hope that others will do likewise.

Shofar

A common quail draws up a worm
that the autumn rain brought to the surface.
This field is edged by a forest
broken only by a single road.
The bird sings *wet-my-lips*
as the worm slips over its white chin
and down its curved black throat.

This stretch to the shetl is pockmarked
with lies and truths, all kicked through
the mud so no one can differentiate:
Trochenbrod, Trochinbrod, Zofjowka.
A place once fought over now razed
with only memory to site it.

There was a post office over there
when it was connected to the world
and debts and love letters hurtled along.
There was neither deliverance nor deliveries,
all correspondence left hanging:

Write back my love ... I'll see you soon ...
They have broken through ...
... Don't return home, we are in Donetsk.
... Turn back!

They are putting up a sign, a memorial plaque
but what good are signs without people
to explain them, to roll up sleeves?

Here dreamer, this is my number
in a sequence of redacted numerals.

But numbers and scale are not the only thing
that should horrify us; it is when we dig deep
and find one femur with growth left in the marrow.

Listen long and you can hear the echo of the Shofar,
its pitch essayed by the player's embouchure,
faithful lips practised in raising remembrance.

Just then the quail takes wing,
winter beckons again tomorrow.

* Trochenbrod (Zofjowka) was completely eradicated in the course of German
occupation and the ensuing Holocaust.

Elijah's Chair
Geneva, 1947

We gathered what and who we could, as lamps
switched with the dawn in watercolour passages.
Beams cut through windows without glass
and through walls gashed and incomplete.

Irina was asked to be the Kvaterin,
a sister to your mother now, having travelled
with us for nearly a year. People coalesce
in groups after every kind of separation.

Uncle Lev forms a chair for you, you settle
in his musician's lap. The Mohel says a few words,
lips crease as the verses come back to him
as if they have never been away.

You are uncovered, I see *zayin*, *dalet*, and *shin*
stamped on the small ivory handled knife.
The blade cuts quick, as if to outrun the pain.
He sucks a line of blood away from the wound.

Your Mother wraps you up quickly. It's January
and the ovens are only starting to warm
for the morning bagels and blintzes, no fresh lox
but we have become used to making-do.

You cry as the drops of wine touch your tongue.
We name you Joseph, after your grandfather.
Your mother and I finish the glass, an unknown
brand that is warm as it goes down my throat.

(III) Tipping Point

Tipping Point

Perching on the partly submerged
shopping trolley, an egret stares down
the length of the shallow canal,

the metal frame cool against his feet,
he shuffles along, algae climbs
up and through the rusting bars.

The sheared bones of branches
exposed last week by the machines
are too short now to bear his weight.

The old water wheel is tarnished to a stop
as pale scum gathers on the river steps, water
flowing slowly has a darker momentum.

The egret watches, pawing at where he stands
and it unnerves me, this doubt of one
who has always known trust in seasons.

With a brain about the size of a plum,
has he enough room for a gram of regret,
a pang that would leaden his wings?

High Tide

For Sian

We stand at the top of the play frame
holding toy binoculars, steering wheels
that turn no physical ship, looking out to the sea.

Silver slides and climbing ropes point to escapes
yet I linger on the horizon, the high grey swell
rumbling as if ready to swallow whole.

Behind me seafront guesthouses sleep,
generations that faced the mighty sea
over tea, toast, a morning paper, now gone.

Gulls hover above us, as if by God's
invisible strings, waiting for prey,
the dive into the blue to eat.

I lift you onto the seesaw. We go up
and down, each time the weight
shifts more to your side.

The Groynes

We gather in the long shore drift,

                pieces of material on the whim,

      coke bottles,
crisp packets,
        condoms,
        caught by the rotting wooden arms
        Man has thrust out into the ocean.

We build loose land together,   grain by grain,
        smoothing out the edges.

We long to be settled,
        but each tide brings more arrivals,
        takes others away.

A Bind of Salmon

Gold inlay with a sovereign face of silver,
you turn the newly pressed pound coin
between thumb and forefinger,
trusting in the revolving frame's revision.
I watch the river, urged onward by nature
to follow every meander of its course
and the fish arrive as one to stake their future,
to take on the clear current's force.

They rush to catch the olfactory memory
and jostle towards the place to jump,
every sinew in forward reverie,
brim-full bodies in full-blooded shunt.
It takes them clear of their own context
to glide for a moment in a gasping heaven,
believing there is something better next,
committing fins and scales to intercession.

I adjust the aperture to frame the leap,
see how Percy Metcalfe designed the mint
of first the Florin coin, then the twenty pence.
How he caught the salmon in a glint and twist
of the late autumn sun, hurtling to lay eggs
so generations would push through the reeds,
stronger but more yielding, supple in the bend,
flashing both past and future in their iridescence.

Open Tuning

He slipped into Donegall Quay, Belfast, night
fading away into an escalating light,
a Harmony guitar from a Sears
catalogue slung over his shoulders.
He played for loose change in the bars
until everything came down about his ears,
returning home, rocking up on foreign land.

I found it gathering dust upstairs
among clothes we used to wear.
Fashion changes, incidentals become
part of the new keys that we hum;
hold shapes, strum the best of the past.
The wood is scratched but these strings last,
still ring out, held in tune by white pegs.

Before the Coffee Kicks In

Eight-oh-five, just the primal
thirst in my widening mouth,
tendons reacting to the lighting.
The shop windows of the arcade
are a dim aquarium, vigourous silver fish
wiggle through the Monday water of
Great Victoria Street station. They jostle
and push each other along with thoughts
of start times and deadlines.
I exit the station and watch a flock
of umbrellas take flight, banking in formation
to evangelize the city with routines.
I tune out the elephants of traffic and
hum my own scandalous innocence,
drawing dirty looks from default faces.
I rub the bristles of my chin
with my opposable thumb, a few grey hairs
poke through, I really should shave.
I enter the coffee shop and gasp out my order,
realising as the brown liquid earths me,
I don't appreciate my thoughts enough.

Mouth of the Ford

The tour bus rumbles down Castle Street,
the ground beneath us calls out in the tongue
of the Farset river, stammered by stone.

High Street paved over the forgotten quaysides
where the merchants first traded the city's name,
the world in reach on the stretching sea.

The Albert Clock is stabilised now but still slightly
off a clear vertical. Built on reclaimed land, listing
from the measurable truth one foot at a time.

Bridges are thrown up one on top of the other,
each generation's ante seen in the engineering,
the reuse of materials to join the unmoving banks.

Samson and Goliath hang questions in the air
in a conversation stalled in awe; the refrain
is that of the sweat-riveted dock days,

sending the world the leviathans of their labours,
Oceanic, Britannic, Celtic... this a city known by
its balancing act on ever-moving currents.

Surface Water

The dawn after the rain leaves
more reflections in the puddles
on Belfast streets in February.

The refuse collectors are an hour
into their work, the baristas warm up
the machines, wipe the countertops.

His body doesn't react to the sound
or bristles of the automotive sweepers
and their mechanical cleansing.

A sleeping bag is curled in a ball.
The label says *Ultra Lightweight,*
Skin Friendly Lining, Synthetically Filled.

Natural causes the paper says,
nothing suspicious, bouquets
are strapped to the railings again

quenching thirst with sheared roots.

Election Night

There were lovers once who thought they were alone
one night in the Glasgow School of Art.

Reckoned that only they could take a palette knife
to scrape off their sfumato surfaces,

find each other underneath as blank canvases willing
to create something out of their vigourous skin,

seek purchase in grams-per-square-metre depth
as they try to fill every gasping fibre.

I had never seen them together before, it was possibly
a grab for the last copy of a book on Warrender.

A *cute meet* they call it in film, and they talked in tongues
as they tried to find a word for *No*, while their lips said *Yes.*

I watched them spill, brush drying in my hand, the piece
I had been working on all night, cinders

already in my jealous eyes, I longed to be in their place —
simple palettes of pink flaming against indigo night.

On Oresund Bridge

There is a need to be joined: this body of water
should not lie between us when we can see
each other's coasts, the blue giving way to green.
Sixteen kilometres of human endeavour going over
and under water, the line to Scania a curved thought
speeding steel through sky before plunging into the sea.
We met in a new millennium, numbers counted down,
balloons rose, we surged in the white promises of New Year.

We said we would call, and did for a few weeks,
sweet nothings kept us talking but also filled the space
with an all too familiar waltz. Oh how we laughed
that my O's were scored and yours had eyes or dots,
a pair of wandering exclamation marks, our tongues
so close but still completely different. I study barnacles
on the undersea columns of the bridge, creatures sure
this handiwork of man would remain permanent.

The bridge has been open for weeks and we can be
together in less than an hour from door to door
but I sit with the ignition off, watching traffic stream
across; a nuclear family away for their holidays,
an old couple visiting Malmö, perhaps for the first time,
a Volvo of students coming the other way to conquer
Europe with just their youth and I wonder if I should,
or can, let that night remain just that night.

Amphorae, Aphrodite, Aghagallon

It is the fine bristles that take each layer off,
revealing a little backstory each time
the brush goes back and forth.

The jars are broken in many parts, possibly
a swish of a dress off the edge of the table.
I bag up the alabaster shards, imagine its shape.

I take samples of the hardened garum paste
then find a rough pestle centimetres away
as if it just finished preparing the evening feast.

Steps attempt to go to a level that no longer exists,
worn perhaps by the sandals that made that trip, I pass
the outline of a bath, see gaps where the pipes went.

A head and torso of what we think is Aphrodite
keeps me company as she waits for the rest
of herself to be unearthed, blank eyes looking upward.

Truncated walls that once dominated the horizon
at their height are scant cover for the wind,
whistling in the depression we have dug up.

Two skeletons form a lattice, off-white frames
embrace, filled with centuries worth of clay and soil,
a ruthless use of space, of who they once were.

It was only last week that you left the papers,
pen already clicked, a pugio dagger on the page,
stickers to point to where to cut my name.

The day you left I watched a documentary
about a long-haired man failing to contain
the excitement of his divining rod, oscillating

over a field that had been fallow for some time,
thinking there was something there.

China Shop

The bulls are running, clearing
the streets of Pamplona,
hooves a hard rain on cobbles.
I track them from my balcony,
people jostle in wine-streaked
shirts, twirl straw hats, plastic cups
are trampled in the crush. A girl
in the crowd looks up, not to see me,
not to see anyone, but it is as if she
has just realised what this is, what it is
all about and her soft face is creased
with epiphany. I want to find out
what truth swims in those porcelain eyes.

Marmalade for John

He comes in and sits down at the same seat,
the one with the plump chintz cushion.
His wife hands him his newspaper,
places down a cup of molten black coffee
on a trembling saucer.
He reaches for the jar of homemade
marmalade, his eyes linger over the
bottling date, written by her once florid hand.
He checks it every day.
He quickly unscrews the lid and places it
beside his plate, picks up his knife
and plunges in.
He watches the jelly blob slowly
slide down the knife
and with one deft manoeuvre
spreads it over the toast.
Undulating mountains of shredded Seville oranges
cover the slice, reaching the neat corners
until a tangerine tangent hangs
precariously above the table,
before it can fall, he takes a bite,
Hmmm delectable preserve, dear.
She nods, takes her seat at the opposite end of the table,
glad as he opens his newspaper.

(IV) The Founds

The Founds

The walls are thick because they need to be,
only the brick to keep out the cold,
rooms darkened by the small windows,
low ceilings, the smoke that talked
from a long-slacked fire.
I touch the tilly lamp as if it could summon stars
with its night jacket of dust and its lack of fuel.
My breaths halo like the smoke rings
my grandfather spun from pursed lips
as he sat in the new house where my mother was born,
just across the yard from this place.
Old tins, cans, oxidised brown clutter this old mantel,
a draft excluder once a patterned snake torn by vermin,
the white stuffing wounds threaded thin on the floor,
things that were left to be forgotten.
My grandfather grew up here;
a hallway too low for him to draw his full height,
no separate bedrooms, no corners to hide in,
if you kept secrets you kept them a long time.
He tilled the fields under open sky,
knew every inch of earth,
claimed and reclaimed with each pre-dawn step
what had been passed from his father,
without ceremony but not without weight.
I try to imagine him at night,
folding into his place in that small bed,
happy to be tired from the day,
quickly falling asleep, sparks
spitting out from the hearth
cooling on his dreams.

Seskinore

She might not make it much longer
my mother tells me,
a refrain that keeps repeating
from the slip road at Craigavon
to just past Seskinore.
Seskinore is somewhere I've never been,
the name a distraction on my tongue.
If I have time I might drive through
on the way back,
to see if it's how I imagine.

We meet outside the nursing home,
you preparing me,
You'll notice quite a difference in her.
Not an admonishment
but I haven't visited for such a long time.
Through the window I can see the River Camowen flow past,
as an upright piano sits lid closed,
a hymnal perched open at *How Great Thou Art.*
She was half-hidden by the armchair,
a faint sketch of her strength,

the woman who delivered babies,
taking small spoonfuls of yoghurt
from nurses whose mentors
she may well have taught.
She recognises me and then doesn't.
Did various faces run across mine
like washing currents? One second me
the next my uncle, all the way back
to people only she would have known.
I become who she needs me to be.
I'll call you if anything changes.
I get back into the car, stir the ignition,

check the fuel gauge as the needle wavers
somewhere between empty and full,
enough to cover the distance.

I pass pylons, staked deep in the fields
to keep the further-out connected
with the rest. I pass the sign for Seskinore
just as the rain comes on. I continue straight on
until I take the exit for home.

View from Gullfoss

We are in the Golden Circle, you and me,
treading the path around Gullfoss,
the steps of others have ascended to the sky,
the ground welcomes our temporal fuss.
I'm not as fit as I used to be,
sweat coats me as I watch so much water
pour itself over the shelf.
The view is so uncluttered up here,
I can see both ends of a rainbow,
but I have no need now of gold or folklore.
I see how light blue threshes to white
as it gate-crashes the pool below
and how all the things that worried us
are not visible from above,
they are not even whispered
there is just the roar of all our names in love.
Can you see it?
Can you see it from where you are?
Whether we speed up the playback
or try to put this moment on pause
everything refreshes then proceeds to the sea,
even my white-knuckled grief needs to go over the falls.
This urn in my hand empties,
the ashes become small black birds flying off
and you, you are then mist.

Traybakes

I never eat them myself but I always pit
glacé cherries in the marshmallow
and digestive biscuit mix, they stick

to my knucklebones as I knead and roll,
desiccated coconut coats the surface
but today licking fingers seems sacrilege.

In the fridge chill a tray of caramel squares,
from the hall the landline trills,
I let the stoic machine pick up the calls.

Pages of recipes litter the counter,
lists of ounces, where and when to cut,
how long to leave anything on the cooling rack.

Clingfilm covers griddle scones and cakes,
a translucent skin so everything is seen,
grieving needs fed with fresh food.

I take out the caramel squares and slice
four lines across and three down,
smaller squares than I'm used to,

many will come,
the wake is tonight,
these were his favourites.

Ribbons

I don't know why I keep it
this powder blue ribbon
that once wound round my ankle
that now can't meet round my wrist.
Did my mother sew and therefore
had the material lying around?
Was it hacked off a curtain tie?
Every time she drew close the drapes
she saw and felt my absence.
The lady at the home said
there was a box full of them
and other mementos of lives
that could have been:
fuchsia, duck egg blue, scarlet,
a miniature bunting parade.
She picked up a rattle, sterling silver
but with the provenance scored out,
a handkerchief with 'A' stitched in the corner,
neatly folded never used to clear
away a runny nose or wipe away
the cake batter after making madeleines.
But it was mostly ribbons, twisting
to find purchase, to attach,
all waiting for someone
to return to collect us like parcels left
at the wrong address overnight.

Brood

Murlough sand gets under my fingernails
as I collect mussels from the wet beach,
forsaking those dragged out, out of reach.
I must make do with those now in my pail
for tomorrow steeps in another low tide.
My fingers pry in the opening of the valves,
testing the shutting of the two hinged halves,
their shells are longer than they are wide.
Buyers fill up their morning stores of brine,
quickly breaking the byssal threads hold,
secrets seep out and the stories unfold
to be skinned with a film of garlic and white wine.
Those I am unable to sell at market find space
on shelves near plant pots, grass seed,
a red-rusted transplanter. I feel the need
at night to come and trace each unviable face.
When young, I briefly held a baroque pearl,
imagined a name was etched in the scry
of its damp nacreous surface swirl,
before the sea made me say: *Goodbye.*

Hearth
For Rhonda

I make a fire for you,
clean the grate
so fresh air can circulate,
lay kindling sticks
for a solid base, rip
firelighters into sugar
cubed accelerants.
I run the red head
of the match along
the striking surface,
it sparks then flares.
I let it come
towards my fingertips
press it to the ready pyre,
watch it tremble
and catch hold.
I add the coals
so the young flame
smokes, burns for longer.
All is ash eventually,
let's not waste our time
being cold.

The Illuminated Manuscript
Trinity College Library 2016

Illustrations entwine like lovers limbs,
colouring across the Chi Rho page;
an otter's teeth redden on a fish,
a peacock is touched with divine ink and fans out his plumage.
Two small mice rage over the Eucharistic host
while two cats keep their claws closed but close,
there is much here for all to eat.
My eyes continue to sweep along
the spine of calligraphy,
ligatures in black, red,
purple and yellow, pulse
on the aged calf vellum, all kept under glass.
There are conversations around
and under the panes, thin places
where heaven and history whisper here and now.
I begin to pick out sacred words in ancient rubrics,
loops on spools that tell of love that died to show itself,
word is made flesh and with it the dust and divine intersect,
angels look on from the edges.
There is something holy in our gaze,
when we seek it we can see the unseen.
I notice others approach,
watch their faces brighten in the beholding.
I step away burdened with light,
grafted to the beckoning vine;
it tells me eternity is in my eyes,
and each eye that was, and is, and will be.

In Places with Two Names

A bilingual sign stands, concreted
into the earth,   staking a double claim.

Black paint violently redacts the foreign wording
        but it still says

        Welcome to /
        Fáilte go.

The most dangerous heresy is the one
a single step away from what we know.

At times two places pass each other seamlessly
as streets,
    schools,
sports,
section lives
        so they don't touch.

But sometimes we meet
        in the larger conversations

        holding a truth in each hand

in a land everyone calls
        home.

Fixing the Power Lines

Parked on the verge, I wrap my utility belt
around my straining waist. I start to climb
the thin rungs. Friesian cows lying in the field,
resigned or unknowing of their fate, watch me
as they slowly make cud. The oak telegraph pole
clasps the steel that harnesses these coils
of electricity, a colossus holding two sides
of a tug of war at once, not losing, not winning.
I pass posters left up from last May's election,
nailed in place in this totem pole, each print
having been briefly higher than the others.
I take my wire cutters, shear them off, watch
faces of Sinn Féin, DUP, UUP, SDLP, Alliance
flutter to the ground, they make no sound now
lying in the ditch. I find the fault and it's easily fixed,
I flick the switch, not simply the source of power
but the intention; zero turns to one, the lights
come on as the lines go live, signal fires spread
out towards a city in the distance, a single glint
becomes a blaze.

Dream Feed
For Cain

A wide open mouth, mostly gums
except for the two small teeth
chuckling a future excerpt.

He giggles at the absurdities
of life reverberating around
the walls he calls his own.

These bright colours that spin
and squeak, objects of textures
and surprises and loud noises.

Slap and suck of the nipple,
the full swirl mouthful,
eyes closed and trusting.

The images that come sharpen
each night, the depth increases
with every minute, he sups

for him every circle still ripples out.

The Song

The evening headlines resonate like gongs — *Terror! Scandal!*
Cat Skateboards! We choose the key to tune to.

I turn the television off and holster the remote down the side
of a well-worn settee, children's socks lie noisily on the floor.

I lock up the front and back doors then slowly ascend
the stairs turning lights off with soft plastic clicks as I go.

I brush my teeth as routine, gargle some mouthwash,
stare at the whistling gap where my molar used to be.

I check in on my daughter, watch her chest rise and fall and rise...
kiss her forehead and pull the blanket up to her chin.

My wife and son are already asleep in the bed and Moses basket,
I creak in and read a little crime fiction, then flick off the light.

I sink down and listen: mother and son breathe in unison,
my daughter harmonises through the monitor.

I close my eyes to join in on this thankful chorus.

ACKNOWLEDGEMENTS

Acknowledgements are due to the following publications in which versions of these poems first appeared: *Southword, Blue Nib, Laldy, Stony Thursday Book, Open Ear, Live Encounters, The Fenland Reed, The Irish Literary Review, The Bangor Literary Journal, The Luxembourg Review, The Incubator Journal, Community arts Partnership Anthologies: Matter, Connections and Resonance.* A selection of poems was shortlisted for The Mairtín Crawford Award.

'The Lotus Gait' won the Seamus Heaney award for New Writing in 2017. 'Fixing the Power Lines' was shortlisted for the 2016 Seamus Heaney Award. 'Zion' won the 2018 Jonathan Swift Creative Writing Award. 'Finding the Water Cold' was shortlisted for The Doolin Writers' Weekend. 'View from Gullfoss' won 2nd place in the Yeovil Poetry Prize. 'The Illuminated Manuscript' won 2nd Place in the 2018 Bailieborough Poetry Prize. 'Brood' won 2nd Place in the Padraic Colum Poetry competition. 'Open Tuning' won 2nd place in the Glebe House Poetry competition. 'Seskinore' was shortlisted in the Red Line Poetry Competition. 'A Young Boy Gathers Sugar, Lancashire 1770' was shortlisted for the Leeds Peace Poetry Prize. 'Marie Tussaud Preserves the Line of Succession' was shortlisted for Hungry Hill's Poetry Meets Politics. 'Ribbons' was shortlisted in the 2018 Clodhorick Poetry Competition. 'The Bridesmaids of Passchendaele' was shortlisted for the Wells Festival of Literature. 'Angelshare' appeared on the inaugural curation of the Poetry Jukebox. 'A Line of Hawthorns' was nominated for the 2016 Forward Prize. 'Taking Soup' was highly commended in the 2016 Gregory O'Donoghue Poetry Competition.

I would like to thank John Walsh, Lisa Frank, Ruth McKee and Tríona Walsh at Doire Press for their invaluable skill and help in putting this collection together. I am grateful for the support of the Arts Council of Northern Ireland, the National Lottery and Damian Smyth. I would also like to thank Colin Dardis and Michael Guiney for their advice and feedback on these poems at various stages. And last but not least my patient wife, Rhonda for her encouragement, love and support.

GLEN WILSON lives with his wife, Rhonda and two children in Portadown, Co Armagh. He is a civil servant and Worship Leader at St Mark's Church of Ireland, Portadown. He studied English and Politics at Queens University Belfast and has a Postgrad Diploma in Journalism Studies from the University of Ulster. In 2014 he won the Poetry Space competition and was shortlisted for the Wasafiri New Writing Prize. He won the 2017 Seamus Heaney Award for New Writing and the 2018 Jonathan Swift Creative Writing Award. In 2018 he was shortlisted for the Mairtín Crawford Poetry Award and was highly commended in the iYeats Poetry Competition. He has also been longlisted and commended in The National Poetry Competition, The Plough Prize, Segora Poetry Competition and the Welsh International Poetry Competition.

www.glenwilsonpoetry.wordpress.com
Twitter: @glenhswilson
Facebook: glenhswilson@facebook.com